Dear Nan and Gra

very much for ei
both do for, me Your encouragement
and guidance help me to be person
I am, without you I would be lost!

Thanks again!
Lots of Love
Rachael xxx

2001: A POETRY ODYSSEY NEWPORT

Edited by Simon Harwin

First published in Great Britain in 2001 by
YOUNG WRITERS
Remus House,
Coltsfoot Drive,
Peterborough, PE2 9JX
Telephone (01733) 890066

HB ISBN 0 75432 988 7
SB ISBN 0 75432 989 5

FOREWORD

Young Writers was established in 1991 with the aim to promote creative writing in children, to make reading and writing poetry fun.

This year the 2001: A Poetry Odyssey competition again proved to be a tremendous success with over 50,000 entries received nationwide.

The amount of hard work and effort put into each entry impressed us all, and is reflective of the teaching skills in schools today.

The task of selecting poems for publication was a difficult one but nevertheless, an enjoyable experience. We hope you are as pleased with the final selection in *2001: A Poetry Odyssey Newport* as we are.

CONTENTS

Bassaleg Comprehensive School

Natasha-Louise Huxtable	1
William Williams	2
Emma Malcahy	3
Gareth Alred	4
Jessica Simmonds	5
Anthony Brown	6
Jocelyn King	7
Alex St John	8
James Gallagher	9
Beth Evans	10
Matthew Wilkinson	11
Claire Barker	12
Kate Whittaker	13
Thomas Beer	14
Claire Thompson	15
Edward Fox-Smith	16
Andrew Kings	17
Elizabeth Stephens	18
Stephanie McDonnell	19
Rhys Jenkins	20
Tomas Forsey	21
Jennifer Mack	22
Elinor Perrin	23
Bethan Cable	24
Simon Shelford	25
Aneira Beament	26
Richard Winter	27
Naomi Denham	28
Thomas Benjamin	30
Katherine Thomas	31
Joseph Dooher	32
Beanish Khan	33
Alex Crocker	34
Alex Hartland-Jones	35
Michael Peck	36

James Fletcher 37
Rachel Williams 38
Amy Lougher 39
Tanya Patrick 40
Victoria Stephens 41
Louise Hall 42
Alexander Price 43
Ahmed Javed 44
Christopher Lewis 45
Anna Mansour 46
Abbie Matthews 47
Earam Tahir 48
Jemma Groucott 49
Alysia Bowen 50
Hannah Ross 51
Hannah Rees 52
Rachel Scrivens 53
Kelly Sibthorpe 54
Thomas Strong 55
Lucy Ambrozejczyk 56
Reema Menta 57
Bethan Jenkins 58
Andrew Kay 59
Nicholas Waters 60
Tom Whitcombe 61
Louisa Lomas 62
Louise Coldrick 63

Bettws Comprehensive School
Tracy Lord 64
Matthew Fife 65
Haydn Farr 66
Angela El-Awiny 67
Richard Cleak 68
James Leadley 69
Casey Hooper 70
David Perryman 71
Samantha Johnson 72

Denise Savage	73
Tiffany Hughes	74
Louise Michelle Ainscough	75
Alexandra Rappell	76
Tania Nelson	77
Matthew Lane	78
Daniel Lewis	79
Samantha A Jones	80
Michala Meadows	81
Hayley Armstrong	82
Emma Brown	83
Kylie Murray	84
Jay Mitchell	85
Emily Benford	86
Adam J Wilkins	87
Hannah Desmond	88
Adele Croker	89
Andy Fussell	90
Ashley G Grant	91
Vikki Sheppard	92
Lianne Sheppard	93
Beth Savage	94
Lauren Couch	95
Gareth Jones	96
Louise Howes	97
Hayley Morgan	98
Amy Cousins	99
Lucy Marsh	100
Rachael Edwards	101
Simon Harvey	102
Lauren Brown	103
Adam Levi	104
Rebecca Jones	105
Amanda Wray	106
Nathan Shepherd	107
Matthew Welsh	108
David Ramsay	109
Karla Skillern	110

Charlotte Vigar 111
Adam Mathlin 112
Ross Yhnell 113
Benjamin Goldsworthy 114
Jennifer Willetts 115
Hannah Parfitt 116
Sarah Baulch 117
Becky Johnson 118
Vicky Howells 119
Sasha Wainfur 120
Ceri Jones 121
Gemma Bartlett 122
David Tutton 123
Alex Coggins 124

Duffryn High School
Charlotte Howard 125
Gemma Preece 126

Newbridge Comprehensive School
Ceri Morris 127
Matthew Thomas 128
Emily Gilbert 129
Claire Williams 130
Lauren Hockey 131
Rachael Keeble 132
Jessica Gibbons 133
Samantha Chivers 134
Zoe Edwards 135
Cathy Parker 136
Owain Millard 137
Kieran Gingell 138
Liam Sheppard 139
Curtis Rundle 140
Alison Dennehy 141
Nicholas Lewis 142
Mathew Gajda 143
Andrew Rogers 144

Nichola Bryant	145
Ffiona Clark	146
Laura Rees	147
Hannah James	148
Joseph Ashford	149
Lauren Hughes	150
Hannah Louise Brown	151
Jessica Dee Walker	152
Scott Symons	153
Sean Price	154
Rhodri Hughes	155
Adrian Yemm	156
Cerys Barrett	157

St Joseph's High School

Laura Fry	158
Marc Wilson	159
Lee Drew	160
Emma Wilson	161
Natasha Milliken	162
Emily Rayment	163
Bethan Tempest	164
Sarah Appleton	165
Sian Manship	166
Matthew Bolton	167
Gregory Walker	168
Alex Driscoll	169
David O'Neill	170
Heidi Northover	171
Bethany Davies	172
Sophie Burridge	173
Danielle Tyler	174
Catherine Jones	175
Rikki Cooke	176
Jordan Bartlett	177
Mariam Bidhendy	178
Deborah Forrester	180
Michael Beirne	181

Sarah Carr   182
Shane Laida   183
Joanne Davies   184
Daniel Stephens   186
Thomas Walker   188
David Whitfield   190

The Poems

SCHOOL DAYS

On Monday :
I had art, made a
masterpiece but fell
apart.

On Tuesday:
I had RS there was no
teacher, so we made a mess.

On Wednesday :
I had PE, I tried to do
a tuck jump but I
sprained my knee.

On Thursday :
I had guidance. I wouldn't
answer her question, so the
teacher made me a dunce.

And on Friday :
I had chemistry, we did
some experiments but
it wasn't as much fun as
dissecting a heart in
biology.

These are my days of school,
I'm all worn out so all I'm going
to do is relax and be cool.

Natasha-Louise Huxtable (12)
Bassaleg Comprehensive School

STORM

The wind began to whistle,
And the grey clouds enclosed,
The shattering hail came thundering
Down like millions of little stones.
There was coldness all around us.
The sea began to crash and wave,
The greyish sky began to attack us
With their ear-piercing thunder that
crackled into a million voices.
The heat has risen,
Suddenly the attacking pitch forks
Stopped and everything fell into pitch
Silence . . .

William Williams (11)
Bassaleg Comprehensive School

SNOW

A magnificent orange and red sun appeared,
Into the soundless sleepy morning of winter,
Turning the sky a heavenly pink.

Glistening grass in the early hours of the morning,
Like icy fingers have walked over it,
Leaving it in a white netting, that is melting slowly away.

People outside laughing and playing,
In a world that was so soundless and so sleepy,
Yet people are taking over it like intruders.

Children slipping and stumbling on patches of ice
Then standing back up and throwing snowballs, at each other,
In the swirling snow.

Trees without leaves strung with cobwebby snow,
Shimmering like glitter,
Make the whole scene a Christmassy one!

Emma Mulcahy (12)
Bassaleg Comprehensive School

SNOW

I love snow,
Falling softly and silently
To the ground,
Piling up high.

Playing snowballs,
Building snowmen,
Running round,
Leaving footprints.

Sledging down hills,
Across the smooth snow,
Faster and faster,
I love snow.

Gareth Alred (11)
Bassaleg Comprehensive School

RAIN POEM

The room suddenly went dark,
Crash, bang.
Lightning lightened up the sky,
The rain drummed upon my window,
Water built up on the ground,
Like the ocean it grew higher and higher,
Then came the thunder, *bang.*
1, 2, 3, 4, 5 miles away.
Then it suddenly just stopped,
Like nothing happened, the water disappeared
The thunder stopped,
The storm was over.

Jessica Simmonds (11)
Bassaleg Comprehensive School

THE STORM

Storm clouds gathering
Growing gloom,
Lightning flashing,
Thunderous boom.
Wind is howling,
Rain is pouring,
Through the night,
The storm is roaring.
Lightning stops,
Wind is dropping,
Getting brighter,
The storm is stopping.
Then silence,
Peace at last,
Calm returns,
The storm has passed.

Anthony Brown (12)
Bassaleg Comprehensive School

HAIL

Bouncing, pounding hail,
Stinging the eyes of innocent children.

Bouncing, pounding hail,
Smashing against frostbitten legs.

Bouncing, pounding hail,
Bashing against the windows of lonely houses.

Bouncing, pounding hail,
Splattering mud in all directions.

Bouncing, pounding hail,
Covering the ground in a blanket of crystals.

Bouncing, pounding hail,
Gathering on the roofs of city slums.

Bouncing, pounding hail,
Cruelly stripping trees of their leaves.

Bouncing, pounding hail,
Ceasing to a silent sun.

Jocelyn King (11)
Bassaleg Comprehensive School

STORM

There is a dangerous stillness in the air.
The last patch of deep turquoise sky is consumed by a grim, hazy,
Solitary cloud,
And, reinforcing this dark omen, a vast rumble proclaims certain doom.
Lightning singes the topmost branches of trees; as they hang helpless.
The sky rattles, rumbles, and roars!
Sodden rain cascades torrentially.

Winds whirl, twist, and gyrate through narrow gorges.
Cruel, jagged, threatening talons rend stark, gaping fissures in the
Chromium horizon.
They stretch hideously, flashing insanely, ripping holes in the air to lash
at the very heavens.
The calamity rages: Lightning flashes, rain pours, thunder bellows,
wind howls.
I am lost. Sodden rain cascades torrentially.

Alex St John (12)
Bassaleg Comprehensive School

TORRENTIAL HAIL

A crescendo comes now from the sky.
The sound of rock-hard hail.
Pinging off metal, pounding the ground.
Shouts and screams of all,
In the storm of *torrential hail!*

Denting car roofs, breaking clay pots,
The downward onslaught goes on.
Playing children have retreated
To their sheltered homes,
Safe from the storm of *torrential hail.*

James Gallagher (11)
Bassaleg Comprehensive School

SNOW SCENE

Fluffy white balls of snow,
Tumble softly down to the ground.
Like soft, broken bits of a ghostly white cloud.
A long. white blanket covers the earth,
Getting thicker every second.
It breaks twigs off bushes and hedges, the strongest trees
Gnarl at the touch.

Each droplet falls as though it has all the time in the world.
Turns cobwebs to pearls, puts twinkling frosty rings
Round a silver moon.
The sky stops showering and the beauty freezes.
The scarlet wintry sun glistening over the scene.

Beth Evans (11)
Bassaleg Comprehensive School

WEATHER POEM

The wind rustles the trees back and forth with ease.
Suddenly a bolt of lightning came down from the
deep thundery sky.
Repeating the lightning a loud bellow of thunder came
out of the sky.
As the storm approaches like a stampede, the thunder gets
deafening, the lightning blinding.
The sky was black, but it's now blue.
The wind stops and it's calm once more.

Matthew Wilkinson (11)
Bassaleg Comprehensive School

ONE COLD WINTER'S NIGHT

Snowflakes fall softly,
Sinking from a royal blue, soundless sky.
Ground smothered in ghostly white, soft,
Smooth silk fabric.
Trees frozen, bare, until the snow covers them
From head to toe.
Street lights shining brightly casting black shadows
On the crystal lined path,
Everything is still.

Children tread cautiously,
Sinking in a deep white duvet.
Scarves and coats pulled tightly round frozen bodies,
Fingers tingling, warm breath helps to relieve the pain.
Kitchen lights beckoning them to come inside.
Everything is still.

Claire Barker (11)
Bassaleg Comprehensive School

THE SUN

The sun shines like a golden sweet wrapper.
It brings warmth and heat to everyone.
The dark grey gloomy scene disappears as the
Sweet wrapper appears slowly.
It glides as slow as slow as can be.
With a shimmer of glitter.
High and higher it rises,
Warmer and warmer the day gets.
The glittering sunbeams bring smiles to faces.
As high noon approaches a great ball of fire emerges from the
Golden sweet wrapper.
We enjoy this time at the beach bathing on the soft summer sands.
The crystal clear waters reflect the ball of fire.
Because fire is hot it brings heat to the water.
The great ball of fire disappears into the golden sweet wrapper.
Still bright,
Still shining,
It fades.

Kate Whittaker (11)
Bassaleg Comprehensive School

THE STORM

First of all calm, calm before the storm,
The gentle breeze gets stronger.
As if something is blowing even harder.
First a soft blow, then a wind, then a gale.
Panic stalks the town like a beast stalks its prey.

Black clouds as dark as death drift above.
The sun is consumed by the cloud's dark jaws.
Forks of light strike.
Engulfing trees and houses in unforgiving, hungry flames.

More strikes follow.
Thunder crashes like huge explosions and deafens all who hear.
The gale tears at houses.
Hurling trees at cars, decimating them.

The lightning stops and the wind dies down.
But the dead sky still watches.
The eye of the storm is near.
The monsoon began flooding and destroying.
Soon the town is no more.
The evil sky had hit its target.

Thomas Beer (11)
Bassaleg Comprehensive School

RAIN

The gentle pitter-patter of frequent rain,
Trickles down my street in a stream-like way.

Who can predict just when it will stop?
The weather forecast is usually wrong!

Keeping you awake well into the night,
How you just wish that rain would stop!

When the night gives way to the day,
We can all breathe a sigh of relief.
The sun shines brightly,
And the fresh dew glimmers.

Claire Thompson (11)
Bassaleg Comprehensive School

AUTUMN GUSTS

The swishing wind bellows through the town,
sometimes quiet, sometimes loud.
Then silence, as it plans another attack.

The swirling wind makes dogs' hairs stand on end,
sometimes gentle, sometimes forceful.
Then it suddenly settles into no more than a breeze.

The spiralling wind turns into a tornado,
sometimes beautiful, sometimes devastating.
As it rips everything from its path into the air.

The changing wind from nothing to a powerful natural force,
sometimes weak, sometimes strong,
It's the same swirling, spiralling, swishing wind.

Edward Fox-Smith   (11)
Bassaleg Comprehensive School

THE STORM

Crashing and splashing goes the rain,
Children rushing inside their cosy homes,
Grown-ups under their umbrellas walking the dog.

The lightning as bright as the sun,
Any second now it could strike a tree.
Wreaking havoc on the community.

The thunder roared after the strong lightning,
Babies crying as loud as a volcano erupting,
The thunder powerful and deafening.

Andrew Kings (12)
Bassaleg Comprehensive School

AN AUTUMN DAY

The wind whistles through the stretched arms of the trees,
It rustles the long strands of my hair,
And my clothes which are bound around my shivering limbs,
Leaves float about like bubbles in the air.

The cold creeps silently round me
And the dew on the grass sparkles in the dim light of day.
I battle with the wind as I walk on and on
And as I enter the warmth of the silent school building,
I sigh with great relief.

Elizabeth Stephens (11)
Bassaleg Comprehensive School

THE STORM

The rain hammers down on the roofs of the houses,
Then noisily runs down the drain pipes,
As the whistling wind rustles the leaves,
And blows over bins, scattering rubbish everywhere.
The sound of a splitting tree, as lightning strikes,
Scaring young children out of their beds,
In the middle of the night.
The loud rumble of thunder,
Like an extremely hungry bear,
Who hadn't eaten for days.
The storm seems to go on forever.

Then as suddenly as it started,
The storm disappears into the atmosphere.
The sound of the hungry bear dies down.
The whistling wind softens, as the lightning stops.
The hammering rain turns into a light drizzle.
The storm is over.
Everything is quiet again.

Stephanie McDonnell (11)
Bassaleg Comprehensive School

SPRING DAY

I look on and on at the cheerful birds speaking their beautiful language.
The air is as clean as a blank piece of paper.
The language of love is filtered through the air as loved ones have been
honoured by Cupid's arrow.

I stop and smell the scent of the plants.
They make me light-headed and loopy as loopy could be.

I then start to have mixed emotions as Spring's distressing rain hits us.
Every thudding raindrop makes a bigger pain in my head.
Suddenly my head stopped pounding as the rain came to a halt and
moved on.

As I gazed on my patio at the sun setting delicately on the horizon, I
watched on and on and on.

Rhys Jenkins (11)
Bassaleg Comprehensive School

THE STORM

The pitter-patter of gentle feet,
As rain splashes down a city street,
As the heart of the storm draws nigh.
Lightning flickers across the sky,
Ever to win the stormy race,
Thunder pushed down to second place.

The clouds thicken, darkness arrives,
With no signs of life anywhere outside.
After raining all night and raining all day;
The rain eventually begins to wane.
Then at last the sky becomes clear,
The end of the storm is finally here.

Tomas Forsey (11)
Bassaleg Comprehensive School

STORM

Sky as dark as the Grim Reaper's cloak,
Lightning as deadly as a newly crafted sword,
Glinting maliciously in the demon's sun,
The thunder rolls on.

Rain like acid eating its way through a stone
Statue of a nation's hero,
Swirling mists of time with the haunted, anguished
Face of those gone before,
Those who had never come back.
The thunder rolls on.

A fork of lightning ripped through the clouds
As a dagger would flash,
I stand petrified, not of the storm but of my own imagination.
The thunder rolls on.

The performance of the elements has reached its climax,
As though it is a gift from God a rainbow breaks evil's reign of the sky,
Like the victory of a blood thirsty battle of good against evil.
The thunder rolls away.

Jennifer Mack (11)
Bassaleg Comprehensive School

STORM CAT

The cat purrs thunderously miles off shore,
Pads towards the little harbour with foamy whiskers.
Boats like hamsters cower under the powerful streaky glare of the
prowler.

He regards the small huddle, his eyes glinting maliciously.
Are these his toys? Or are they his next meal?
He can't decide.

He lifts his paw ready to strike but
Then he turns and stalks away,
Leaving the water as dark as a young girl's forlorn eyes.

Elinor Perrin (12)
Bassaleg Comprehensive School

THE STORM

The lightning stretched its fingers down to earth,
As fishermen watched,
Apprehensive.

As the tempest raged,
The lone figure, trudging slowly through
Darkened streets,
Grew steadily drenched.

The smooth svelte cat, once lazy, relaxed,
Shot into the house,
Terrified.

But the girl, excited and amazed,
Listened to the shout of thunder,
And watched the shadows dance across the
wall.
She was not afraid.

Bethan Cable (12)
Bassaleg Comprehensive School

STORM

All was still,
The air heavy,
The birds silent,
Grey clouds forming.
An eerie light,
Darkness.
A distant rumble,
Was that a flash?

Coming closer,
Echoing,
Getting nearer,
Flashing brighter.
Booming, rumbling.
Even closer.

Lightning slicing clouds,
Hypnotic power,
Holding our attention.
Electric power,
Cutting down trees.
Splitting nerves.
And scaring creatures.
Is it here to stay?

Simon Shelford (11)
Bassaleg Comprehensive School

THE SEA

The sea
A vast square of blue felt
Rolling in and out as it pleases
Swallowing up the sand
As it creeps up the beach
Collecting in pools of rock
Resting its frightening bulk
Flipping fins
Express the feelings within
A ghostly surface
Shimmering in the pale moonlight
Quivering, waiting for sunrise
Withholds the monsters within.

Aneira Beament (11)
Bassaleg Comprehensive School

WHITE -OUT

Shards of icy mist
Engulf my wind-swept face.
Heading into it at speed
It whips my body till it's numb.
Clearing away layers of snow
Revealing bare sheets of ice.
It howls continuously
Like a pack of famished wolves.
It whirls its way
Grabbing humans and animals
Unexpectedly.
A whistling wonder of washed out colour
Glides over deserted peaks.
A blinding light soon emerges
As the snow storm dissolves
Into nothing.

Richard Winter (12)
Bassaleg Comprehensive School

MIST

She sits by the ocean, the waves coming in one by one, and gently
kissing her feet.
Her pale, fragile face, as white as the moon, faces a far-away land
Her eyes, a haunting grey, holding all the secrets of the world, drop
a single pearly tear on her cheek,
She is lost, ran away from home and can never return.
Her clothes, ragged and torn, fly behind her, creating a thick mist for
the world around.
Her silvery hair dances in the wind around her, a cruel wind that hits her
face,
But she cannot see or hear, she is blind to happiness, only sees sadness.

The lady of rain passes through swiftly, waltzing in the breeze,
Her clothes of pearls, drop diamonds that stay to dry up behind her
Her pale blue hair flows out behind her, leaving memories, shattered
into tears.
Mist stays on, reliving her past in her mind.
Lightning appears suddenly, ripping out her golden curls in anger,
She sees Mist, and her eyes light up with cruelty.

A battle begins, Lightning throwing her curls at Mist, ripping Mist's
clothes even more.
Night comes along with Midnight, leaving a trail of magic across the
sleeping land,
The battle goes on, Mist getting weaker by the minute.
Lightning throws her last group of curls, hitting Mist in the chest,
Mist sinks down onto her knees, her eyes filling with tears of pain,
Never getting her last wish; to see her family again.
with one last cry, she closed her eyes.

Every breath drained more life from her body,
At last she lies still, her chest no longer rising and falling,
Lightning melts, satisfied, away into the dawn.

Sun comes out, her golden rays bringing a new morning to the land,
Signalling the end of the battle.

Naomi Denham (12)
Bassaleg Comprehensive School

THE MATCH

Rugby match . . .
A ferocious stag thirsting for a fight,
Steamy scrums clashing with strong antlers
A battle breaking out. A score to settle.
Pentrepoeth 15 - Lliswerry 20

Rugby match . . .
A tamed lion being studied by scientists,
Worried about what they are thinking.
Each player on display - an exhibit of skill to be selected.
Pentrepoeth 25 - Monnow 15

Rugby match . . .
An Olympic final, the one that counts.
Competitors on their marks like starving tigers ready to pounce.
The deep disappointment . . .
Pentrepoeth 20 - Mount Pleasant 20

Thomas Benjamin (11)
Bassaleg Comprehensive School

DAWN

The cockerel crows,
The alarm went off,
The morning had awoke,
The sun beamed through the puffy clouds,
The birds sing their favourite song,
For now it's a brand new day.
Children stretch, yawn and groan,
Tired faces all around,
Washing, changing, breakfast and rushing,
Will they be ready in time?
Grandfather clock strikes, it's eight o'clock,
Time to catch the bus.
The bus stops; they scurry on,
They're on their way to school.
Working hard, time flies,
They've made it through the day!

Katherine Thomas (11)
Bassaleg Comprehensive School

TORNADO

T wirling and twisting
O blivious to its destruction
R eeling and rolling round the sky
N othing left in its path
A nimals soaring through the air
D itching everything it picks up
O rdinary world once again.

Joseph Dooher (11)
Bassaleg Comprehensive School

FIRE

Blazing in gold,
Quenching in red
A red hot flickering flame,
Changing colours time to time,
Ready to eat anything alive
Like a dragon spitting out hoops of blaze,
Hot, hot fire, scorching, burning,
Crackling fire,
Flames drowning, drowning away,
Devouring life slowly dying,
Crackling,
Burning,
Faintly fades,
Flickering flame flickers away
No longer existing,
Ashes of grey still and quiet.

Beanish Khan (11)
Bassaleg Comprehensive School

THE WINTER MOON

The winter moon, shining bright,
Over the hills it comes alight,
Bringing peace to earth as people sleep,
The everlasting glow, until morning it keeps.
Then suddenly it dims as it drifts behind a cloud,
Making the whole world darker all around.
It holds the world in a gentle trance,
The silent stars twinkle and dance,
But after the reign of the midnight sun,
The winter moon, its work is done.

Alex Crocker (11)
Bassaleg Comprehensive School

THE SUN

Burning through the sky,
A giant fireball,
Put there by the greatest dragon,
And will never fall.

Making things look brighter;
Rays dance in the summer breeze,
Cheerful, happy, hopeful,
Glinting off lakes and seas.

The king of the sky sets,
Like butter melting in a hot saucepan,
Much more beautiful than anything,
That can be created by man.

Alex Hartland-Jones (11)
Bassaleg Comprehensive School

AT THE PARTY

People arrived like flocks of sheep.
They crowded round the birthday boy.
Food was carried in on decorated plates.
The birthday boy showed and amazed the other
kids with his toys.
They sat at the table and the birthday boy opened his
presents.
He tore them open wildly and passed the money to his mum.
Then they dived into the food like ravenous dogs.
In no time at all it was gone like it had never existed.
Then came the moment they had all been waiting for.
The cake.
The candles flickered like stars as the lights went off
The familiar tune from many years started.
The birthday song.
As the tune ended he blew the lights out.
Then came the party games.
Pass the parcel and musical chairs.
As darkness crept in people started to leave.
One by one.
Then it was just the birthday boy, his parents and
His presents.

Michael Peck (12)
Bassaleg Comprehensive School

FOOTBALL

I play football on Sundays,
Some we win, some we lose,
Supporters line up on the touchline,
To shout and cheer us on.

My team takes kick off,
And the match is under way,
We run up and down, passing and shooting,
And the ball hits the back of the net.

We high-five one another,
And we're off running again,
Just five more minutes to the whistle,
We must hold on to the ball.

We shout, we've won,
Our shirts are muddy.
And our boots are covered in dirt and mud,
We must have a drink.

James Fletcher (10)
Bassaleg Comprehensive School

A JOURNEY

A stream like a journey,
Flowing through land, as smooth as silk.
Its aim -
To join the greatest place of all.
Starting as a trickle of water,
Journeying on to larger places.
Finally joining the deepest of all,
The depths of the ocean!

Life is a journey,
Moving through the world as we age.
Venturing through school,
Helping us achieve our aims.
Starting as tiny bawling babies,
Gradually discovering the world.
Finally finding ourselves facing the last journey.
The journey of death . . .

Rachel Williams (11)
Bassaleg Comprehensive School

THE CAT

Quietly creeping, silent and slow,
She stalks through the grass,
Head held low.
Body squirming across the ground,
A pause; she pounces!
Her prey is found.

Twisting, turning around a leg,
She jumps for her food
Then sits to beg.
Silently pleading with luminous eyes,
It's hard to refuse
Her persistent cries.

Peacefully purring, contented and smug,
She stretches and yawns,
Curls up on the rug.
Happy to snatch forty winks in the sun
'Til, fully recharged.
She's off for more fun.

Amy Lougher (12)
Bassaleg Comprehensive School

FLOOD!

Gushing water drowns out every other sound,
Not the majestic blue of the sea,
But a dirty, soiled brown,
Non-stop torrential rain rockets down against slated roofs,
Manners of a pig,
This monstrous force barges into every space,
River banks bursting with a silent,
Unknown but stupendous force,
A waterfall of anticipation sweeps across the land,
This unstoppable,
Unlimited amount of water sentences death to harmless things,
Cruelty is its name,
The death door of drowning slowly creaks open,
Water rising,
Slowly seeping peoples lives away,
Animals left struggling,
Frantic,
Against the fast flowing flood.

Tanya Patrick (11)
Bassaleg Comprehensive School

BURNING

I watched silently as my house burned to the ground,
People from the neighbourhood were watching all around.
All my memories were being destroyed as I watched with my own eyes.
Tears trickled slowly down my cheek.
The silence and darkness of the night was destroyed by the thundering fire,
Sweating firemen tried desperately to put it out with a raging river coming from the hose's nozzle.
The feelings inside me grew bigger and bigger!
And 'No!' I shouted, thinking that would stop everything.
But as I turned, nothing had changed,
Five minutes later, there was silence,
Like a classroom full of children when a teacher enters the room,
The fire had vanished,
But so had my home!

Victoria Stephens (11)
Bassaleg Comprehensive School

PHOENIX

I am an omen of prosperity,
A lover of fire,
A bird you won't see,
Well hardly.
I am born again, several times,
I contain Yin and Yang,
Male and female,
My head is the rooster of the sun,
My back the curve of the crescent moon,
My wings are of the wind,
My tail feathers are the trees and the flowers,
My feet the earth,
My plumage blends all colours and,
My call is a sweet harmony of just five notes.

Louise Hall (11)
Bassaleg Comprehensive School

MY FIRST BIRTHDAY

Guests arriving one by one,
The food is uncovered.
Everyone hastens to get there.
Mountains of food, covering faces,
Then nothing.
Where was my mum,
Suddenly she arrives with a huge cake.
What is it?
It had a golden flame flickering.
Soon a roar of 'Blow, blow, blow' Arose.
So I did.
The light knocked down in its prime.
By a violent rush of wind, just killing it.
Then an outbreak of roars came up.
Why so joyful at a tragic event.
Soon everyone was going one by one.

Alexander Price (11)
Bassaleg Comprehensive School

THE FIRE LION

Fire lion, a lion no man can beat,
Because of his burning blazes of heat.
When ready for prey,
Don't get in his way.
And when you hear a roar,
The door of death will be an open door.
Run, run and make like a tree.
For there will be no mercy,
For you are not safe until he comes,
The great comes,
The rain comes.

Ahmed Javed (11)
Bassaleg Comprehensive School

TOY TRAIN

Is it my father?
Is it my father long ago?
Is it my father, finally free!
Is it my father wrapped warmly?
Is it my father with auburn hair, with deep black eyes?
The black deep eyes of his father's pit?
The mining pit of his mind.
The mining pit of his hardness, coldness,
Is it my father by his railway?

Christopher Lewis (14)
Bassaleg Comprehensive School

WHY?

This photo was taken long ago,
In the far off land of my innocent childhood.
But why do so many things have to change?
And why do people have to die?
The lap that I sat on,
But never will again.
That beautiful smile,
Which will never shine again.
Her warm, kind face,
Her comforting embrace.
Why do so many things have to change?

Anna Mansour (14)
Bassaleg Comprehensive School

POLLY

As I stare at the picture of her beautiful face,
I can hear the grateful 'purr' she made,
When I opened the door for her.

She was an unusual creature,
With peach, grey and white fur,
Her eyes were snake-like,
Everyone that saw her would comment,
That made me proud!
She should have been proud too,
With the three adorable kittens she produced,
But not one of them looked like her.

Now she's gone and I miss her,
I miss her annoying habits,
She would eat the cat litter and leave traces
of her different colour hairs on the furniture.
I still find her long, white whiskers,
Sticking out of cushions or in room corners.

Abbie Matthews (14)
Bassaleg Comprehensive School

ALL LOCKED UP

All locked up
an animal in a cage,
nowhere to run, nowhere to hide.
All locked up
like I'm not real,
a toy to be looked at.
All locked up
away from others,
left to live a life like this.
All locked up
having never seen anything,
except the bleak, black walls.
All locked up
here I shall stay,
no one to help me survive.
All locked up.

Earam Tahir (14)
Bassaleg Comprehensive School

UNKNOWN

It was a long time ago
Longer now than it seems
A place that perhaps I have seen in my dreams
One endless obscurity
Of running, playing, laughing and crying
Yet you remain in obscurity to the world
The adult's world
A place you dare not venture
If only I knew what lay ahead
Oblivious of the feelings you'll get
Of love, hate, devotion, regret
Prayer and wishes, scars and kisses
Angels, demons, men, women
What lies ahead?
Ex-boyfriends, next boyfriends
True best friends, new best friends
Familiar faces and foreign places
You don't dare to enter
But long to be a part of it
If only I knew what lay ahead.

Jemma Groucott (15)
Bassaleg Comprehensive School

BEATING FEAR

Presenting fear in my mind the endless track towered above,
Off we went up and up,
A face of terror glanced at me,
I tried to reassure - she seemed to acquiesce,
'Don't look down'
Whoosh - we dropped,
Plummeted to the ground leaving our fears behind.

Alysia Bowen (14)
Bassaleg Comprehensive School

A FROZEN IMAGE

I remember the rain
and the blanket of snow,
grey clouds that filled the sky.
I remember my sister standing next to me
and the tree that we stood next to.
I remember how cold that day was.
I remember my red, glowing nose.
I remember the click of the camera.
I remember who the little girl was
with her red nose
and that long, red hair.
But what happened before
and after that day,
is now forgotten
and a frozen image left in its place.

Hannah Ross (14)
Bassaleg Comprehensive School

THAT SAME OLD SMILE

I can't remember going to the beach on that day,
I can't even remember what happened.
All I do remember are my screams of laughter
And my familiar smile which was never off my face.
My chubby little arms and my chubby little legs.
The Snoopy T-shirt which was growing too small.
The waves of the sea which I jumped over.
My red, raw cheeks which were blazing from the sun.
Although this day is a distant memory,
I still can manage that same old smile.

Hannah Rees (15)
Bassaleg Comprehensive School

MEMORIES

The little girl in the photo is me,
a beaming smile as I pretend to mow the lawn,
with my colourful, plastic lawnmower.
I can't remember that orange, flowery dress.
The sun shone down on the grass of my grandma's lawn,
casting shadows all around me.
A happy picture, even the lawnmower is smiling.
All those childhood memories seem to fade;
as if they had never been.

Rachel Scrivens (14)
Bassaleg Comprehensive School

MY MAKING

Look again, take a glance.
A young girl alongside her best friend.
The sun on their back, the air on their face,
the dew in the meadow, that fresh summer contains.

That pose I remember, as that one click captured, the entire story.
That tree I remember, the one I climbed,
now only a stump is left in ruin
That bench I remember, on the fifth of November,
as we turned it to ash in a ball of fire.

But I do not remember,
I have forgot.
Who is that girl in the snapshot?
Is the question not who she was then?
But who she is now?

She has grown up, her best friend has too
and although they are divided, they are united.
Memories complete, together they hold.
But, now in that picture there would be
another young girl, repeating that past
made by me!

Kelly Sibthorpe (15)
Bassaleg Comprehensive School

A PICTURE OF OLD

This picture!
Where did it come from?
I can vaguely remember this picture being taken.
Is that - no, it can't possibly be!
But yes,
This carefree child,
With nothing to fear,
Is no one but me!
On that bright, red bike,
With the face painted,
Oh, how funny I looked.
That day,
That sun kissed day,
When the orb was fat and soothing.
The child could not have had a care in the world!
No care for war,
For famine,
Or worse still, for homework!
With that unbrushed hair,
That face full of joy,
And that immense smile on his face,
What, but age itself, could change this child from
what he was to the occasional, savage beast
he has become?

Thomas Strong (14)
Bassaleg Comprehensive School

MY POEM

I've done it!
I have emulated the best
I can't quite believe it
Is this my fate?
I knew I could do better
I could have been number 1
Could I stand up to the test?
Can I do everything all at once?
There is a lot of talk about me
Maybe I will, maybe I won't.

Lucy Ambrozejczyk
Bassaleg Comprehensive School

THE BLACK HOLE

Those dark, mysterious eyes
staring at me
Sparkling eyes crowded me
Sharp screams repeating
It's all rushing back
The speed of the trailer
The splutters of water
Bumpy, rocky
Suddenly
Stop!

Reema Menta
Bassaleg Comprehensive School

ANGEL FACE

Is that little angel me?
The apple of my father's eyes,
That face of innocence lost in
A grown-ups' world,
Longing to be part of it.

The mischievous thoughts within that angel's head,
Never to be put into action,
Naïve to the problems of that grown-up world.

Is that little angel me?
The one with the curly locks,
The hazel-brown eyes,
The dummy in the mouth,
Is to be part of that grown-up world.

Bethan Jenkins (14)
Bassaleg Comprehensive School

THE HIDDEN KILLER

He sits there staring at you,
through those caring, loving eyes.
His sweet little face, his fine coat.
Everybody loves him.
But on the other side lurks a dark spirit,
a killer, stalking you watching your every move.
He sits there, his lethal weapons concealed
behind that cute doggie face.
A mere sparkle in his eyes.
Is it man's best friend or is it man's worst enemy?

Andrew Kay (14)
Bassaleg Comprehensive School

THE HEART OF ENGLAND

Yorkshire in the heart of England,
tranquil and at peace.
It's springtime.
Grasses are waking,
stretching out their scrawny necks.
Birds peck at the newly born shoots,
as they break free from the fleshy earth.
Water gushes from the sheer cliff face,
as it tumbles to the valley below.

Nicholas Waters (14)
Bassaleg Comprehensive School

THE MISSING SOUL

Her dark enchanted eyes of dark, long grass,
The embittered smile and those glimmering teeth,
The cold wind gusts through her wavy hair like
the sway of those old, dark, tall trees.
The way she looks is easy to know that she is not herself,
something missing, something vanished.
The picture suggests she's distraught and emptiness is there.
I think of that sad, old woman.
I take into account her heartbreak,
but cannot tell what is missing.

Tom Whitcombe (14)
Bassaleg Comprehensive School

RAF Valley

Here we are, about fifty of us
We came here on a big white bus
We came to march, we came to fly
We came to zoom up in the sky
The Sea Kings hovered and the Hawk Jet soared
It was tiring but we weren't bored
We'd get up at 5.30 every morning
It was cold and we were yawning
But in this picture here we are
We're happier than then by far.

Louisa Lomas (14)
Bassaleg Comprehensive School

WHAT HAPPENED HERE?

A pitiful child sitting there,
Shreds of dew glide down her delicate skin.
Her sorrowful eyes, filled with tears,
Lips quivering, ready to burst.
Candy all around her mouth,
Hides her rosy cheeks.
The look of guilt,
Is carried in the lines of her face.
What did she do?
I wonder!

Louise Coldrick (14)
Bassaleg Comprehensive School

ON THE DAY I WAS BORN

On the day I was born bells rang out.
On the day I was born birds flew into the air.
On the day I was born the stars shone brightly.
On the day I was born the sun was bright.
On the day I was born the moon shined.
On the day I was born planets came together.
On the day I was born an old man found a home.
On the day I was born machines went mad.
On the day I was born babies were sleeping.
On the day I was born rivers raged.
On the day I was born the sea was calm.
On the day I was born the wars were no more.
On the day I was born people sang.

Tracy Lord (14)
Bettws Comprehensive School

FINDALOO!

Hubble bubble, toil and trouble,
Fire burn and toilet bubble.
The other day I had a curry,
And I ran to the loo in an awful hurry.

No 44 or No 66?
Which one will I pick?
The one I picked had chicken, mushrooms and chillies too.
I started at 6 and I finished at 2!

Then one moment there was a roar,
And I couldn't stand it anymore.
It felt worse than diarrhoea,
All the agony in my rear!

Matthew Fife (13)
Bettws Comprehensive School

IF I WAS . . .

If I was a food
I'd be a pizza
People will be
Eating me in Ibiza

If I was an animal
I'd be a shark
Eating people
Called Mark

If I was reincarnated
I'd be Ryan Giggs
I'd own a farm
With lots of pigs

If I was a plant
I'd be a thorn
Stinging people
Till the morn

If I was a car
I'd be a Ferrari F40
High and mighty
Always naughty

If I was a superstar
I'd be Kane
Handing out
A lot of pain.

Haydn Farr (12)
Bettws Comprehensive School

WHAT IS A TEARDROP?

A teardrop
is rain that has
fallen from the clouds
A teardrop is hailstones
belting down from above
A teardrop is an icicle
that has frozen.
A teardrop is a
leaking tap that
hasn't been
turned
off.

Angela El-Awiny (12)
Bettws Comprehensive School

ON THE DAY I WAS BORN

On the day I was born clocks stopped,
On the day I was born planets crashed,
On the day I was born an old man died,
On the day I was born a baby cried,
On the day I was born politicians wined,
On the day I was born an army suffered,
On the day I was born stars brightened,
On the day I was born the sea roared,
On the day I was born the sun exploded,
On the day I was born the moon lit,
On the day I was born bells boomed,
On the day I was born the world began.

Richard Cleak (12)
Bettws Comprehensive School

WHY WAR?

My ears ringing,
birds not singing,
shells going off,
hopes are lost.

I see a man cry,
for his dreams have died,
like so many others,
sprawled across this
field of ash.

This once peaceful
meadow,
full of green grass,
now no more than
mud from blasts
of enemy cannon
fire that
lasts and lasts.

James Leadley (12)
Bettws Comprehensive School

PARENTS

They all have different rules,
They all have different ways,
Some use the belt,
Others use slippers,
Hurts either way,
They all shout and scream,
They all rant and rave,
Some ground us,
Others punish us,
Makes us feel like slaves,
Still we have to thank them,
For food they buy,
For clothes they give,
For everything they do,
Everything we've done,
They've been there.

Casey Hooper (13)
Bettws Comprehensive School

BLACK IS A COLOUR...

Black is the colour
of Dracula's
bride.

Black is the colour
of the darkness
outside.

Black is the colour
of the
Dead Sea.

Black is a colour
that's not
right for me.

David Perryman (11)
Bettws Comprehensive School

THE RAIN

The rain is God crying
When he is sad
Rain is blue diamonds
Falling from the sky
The rain is a cold feeling
A cold type of home
It makes me feel cold.

Samantha Johnson (13)
Bettws Comprehensive School

THE BEACH

Four hours on a train
We've arrived at last
Ready for a perfect day
And forget what's happened in the past.

Riding on a banana boat
With cool icy water underneath
Riding past
The Great Barrier Reef.

Lying on a sandy beach
Laughing with all my friends
Saying this day is already brill
I hope it never ends.

Grabbing an ice-cream
Running to the sea
Down the sandy beach
Shouting, 'You can't catch me!'

Riding on my white horse
Galloping over the waves
Pretending we are cavemen
Exploring all the caves.

Strolling up the beach
With sand all in my hair
Finishing this day
With rides on the fair.

Denise Savage (11)
Bettws Comprehensive School

DOUBLE TROUBLE

Double trouble, toil and trouble,
Fire burn cauldron bubble,
Take an eye of a cat,
Wing of a bat,
A tail of a rat,
End of a mat.

Double trouble, toil and trouble,
Fire burn, cauldron bubble,
A slimy snail,
Tongue of a whale,
Tale of a tortoise,
Leg of a rodent,
Double trouble, toil and trouble,
Fire burn, cauldron bubble . . .

Tiffany Hughes (11)
Bettws Comprehensive School

THE EAGLE

The large eagle flies quietly
Looking for a hopping rabbit
He spots the grass moving
Like a bunch of snakes
And dives like a jet, crashing.

The eagle hunting for its prey
If I'm right, it's been hunting all day
Those dark, brown eyes
The way it flies
Those round curved claws.

Louise Michelle Ainscough (13)
Bettws Comprehensive School

THE HALLOWE'EN FRIGHT

On Hallowe'en the witches come out,
But most of all they wander about.
They wander for the lives of children,
To mix them up in a black cauldron.

They stand around ready to snatch them,
They better find a camouflaged den,
Or eyes of children will be fine,
Better than a glass of wine.

Beware you're in for a *scare!*
Ha, ha, ha, haaa!

Alexandra Rappell (11)
Bettws Comprehensive School

WIND

A wind is a rattle eruption,
it comes from a place called 'bum'.
It rolls down the leg of your trousers
and comes out in a spectacular hum.
It warms the bed in winter,
it suffocates all the fleas.
The motto of this poem
is never eat faggots and peas.

Tania Nelson (12)
Bettws Comprehensive School

ON THE DAY I WAS BORN

On the day I was born, bells rang
On the day I was born, an old man was happy
On the day I was born, an army battled
On the day I was born, the sea waved
On the day I was born, the sun smiled
On the day I was born, stars sparkled
On the day I was born, politicians argued
On the day I was born, the planets collided
On the day I was born, clocks ticked
On the day I was born, a bird sang
On the day I was born, children played
On the day I was born, the moon rose
On the day I was born, rivers roared
On the day I was born, an old woman laughed
On the day I was born, a dog barked
On the day I was born, my dad collapsed
On the day I was born, machines stopped
On the day I was born, aliens landed
On the day I was born, animals howled
On the day I was born, Elvis sang
On the day I was born, I climbed onto my mother
On the day I was born, people cried
On the day I was born, a duck quacked
On the day I was born, a flower blossomed
On the day I was born, schools closed
On the day I was born, the bees buzzed
On the day I was born, animals ran
On the day I was born, the leaves fell
On the day I was born, balloons popped.

Matthew Lane (16)
Bettws Comprehensive School

PLANETS!

The world is spinning,
The planets fly through
With rages of fire,
But as fast as a cockatoo.
Pluto is round, as cold as can be,
As slow as a snail,
But far away from me.
Jupiter is warm, Jupiter is soft,
So please don't go there because
It's like froth!

Daniel Lewis (12)
Bettws Comprehensive School

ZOO ANIMALS

Monkeys, rhinos, lions and snakes
They all live in the wild
The tropical fish swim swiftly in a lake
And the birds glide past in the sky

But now that has changed, they're not so free
They live in loneliness and pain
The monkeys and the bats hang glumly from the trees
And the big cats sleep sadly behind bars

The elephant's trumpet, the lionesses' roar
The penguins waddle across the ice
The keeper comes strolling to the door
. . . But only to leave their food.

They stare at the faces, laughing and joking
They feel their heart heave
They turn their back to people poking
And they wish they were back at home.

Samantha A Jones (12)
Bettws Comprehensive School

DON'T PUT SUGAR IN MY TEA MUM!

Don't put sugar in my tea mum,
Don't put sugar in my tea.
I'm already fat,
So that's enough of that.
Don't put sugar in my tea.

Michala Meadows (12)
Bettws Comprehensive School

DREAM OF A FOREST

Drip, drip goes the water falling from the tree,
Squeak, squeak, ribbit
All the animals that I see
Walking through the forest
All the animals that hear
But for some reason they know I don't fear
Then I see a bird with red and white wings
The melody of its songs it just sings and sings
Then I come to the end of the forest
I look away and around there is no one to be seen
And no one to be found.
All I've seen was a dream.

Hayley Armstrong (12)
Bettws Comprehensive School

HORROR

H orrible, petrifying,
O gre monster, ahhh,
R eaching out to grab me,
R un for your life!
O h no, he's behind me,
R un, run.

Emma Brown (13)
Bettws Comprehensive School

HORROR POEM

He roars in the moonlight
Ripping down trees
He strolls around the woods
Catching passers by
Takes them to the damp, dark cave
Where he ties them to the large wooden pole
He blinds them with a cloth
He then lights the skin
Burning fire around the wooden pole
He then roars loudly
It echoes round the woods
Then with one last look
He leaves you to burn.

Kylie Murray (13)
Bettws Comprehensive School

WATCHING BIRDS

Watching birds
Watching birds
Watching birds
All day

The magpie
Count them - 1, 2, 3
Two love birds
Sitting in a tree

Watching birds
Watching birds
Watching birds
All day

A bright white dove
Overhead
To end a day of
Watching birds!

Jay Mitchell (12)
Bettws Comprehensive School

HORSE RACE

Horses, horses, horses,
Ready to win the courses,
Waiting in a line,
For the right time,
Black horses, brown, white and dun,
Waiting for the starting man with the gun.

Bang!
They're off.

Horses, horses, horses,
Running the race.
In a very steady pace,
The commentator very quick,
Tick, tock, tick.

Horses, horses, horses,
The time is scurrying,
The horses are hurrying,
In the lead is number three,
And close up is Herbal Tea.

Horses, horses, horses,
The finish line is up ahead,
Where the famous Red Rum had lead,
The winner is number three,
Ahead by a knee.

Emily Benford (12)
Bettws Comprehensive School

THE WEATHER

Tears of rain streaming down the eyes of the window,
Everything covered in a layer of clear liquid,
Raindrops diving from spring board leaves,
Soggy post oozing through the letter box as the
drowned postman gets attacked by my dog.

A multicoloured Mardi Gras of umbrellas dancing
down a high street,
Games lessons are cancelled as we are forced
to write lines about fitness,
Dark clouds ominously move towards the
unsuspecting sun, to cover up it smiley face,
Boring bored games forced upon us by Dad,
because we can't go on a 'family drive'.

Puddles provide excellent entertainment for young children,
Puddles provide anger for my mum when I come home muddy.

Adam J Wilkins (12)
Bettws Comprehensive School

SWEETS!

I go to the shop on a day like today,
Shall I buy a Chomp or a Milky Way?
There's lots of different bars to choose,
With loads of candy, I just can't lose.
Smarties, Dimes, Snickers and Polos,
Mars bars, Crunchie, Taz bar and Rolos.
By now I'm getting hungry, hungry for lots,
Lots and lots of Jelly Tots.
I go to reach in my big pocket,
For enough to buy a pack of Lockets.
Honey crumble wrapped in juicy honey,
'Oh my God, I've forgot my money.'

Hannah Desmond (12)
Bettws Comprehensive School

TECHNOLOGY

The Internet is so confusing,
Are the web sites so amusing?
Modem, hard drive is all they say,
I'll stay well out of technology's way.

The mouse, the keyboard and CD-Roms,
Blow them all up with a barrel of bombs.
All the programmes and games,
They drive me insane.

Don't you agree it's all confusing me!

Adele Croker (13)
Bettws Comprehensive School

THE GAME

I like the rain
In the fast lane
Because I am the game.

It's not a matter between you and me
It's not a case of lust you see
It's a matter of you versus me.

They were stepping up the pace
And giving chase
But I won the high speed race.

I really thought I could make you number one
And in time it come
Let's enjoy the fun.

Andy Fussell (13)
Bettws Comprehensive School

MY PERFECT DAY

My perfect day,
Would be in May.
With lots to say,
About the sun's warm ray.

The bees and the birds are flying around.
A nice, calm day, where no clouds are found.
The trees are tall, greener and free,
And people walk steadily with lots to see.
Kids run home after their boring day at school,
They run around cheerfully then jump in the pool.
The air is fresh, the grass is green,
The sky is blue, it's just a dream.

In the warm sapphire night,
The stars are out, the moon shines bright.
So now asleep in bed I lay,
Dreaming of 'my perfect day'.

Ashley G Grant (12)
Bettws Comprehensive School

NIGHT

The moon, the moon
I'll see you soon
The stars tonight
The stars so bright
The black sheet
That is the sky
I wonder where
I wonder why.

Vikki Sheppard (12)
Bettws Comprehensive School

PAIN

Everyone endures some pain,
I hear each life must have some rain.
Everybody seems to think,
That they get the worst of it.
You wonder why there are people,
Who couldn't really care.
If your life's been much worse than theirs.
But why?
Everybody is ignoring your pain . . .
Because they're too busy with their own.

Lianne Sheppard (14)
Bettws Comprehensive School

FAT

They call me fat
But I can't help it
I'm bigger than average

I'm on a diet
I feel so hungry
So hungry I could faint

I've lost 10 stone
My hair's all limp and lifeless
My face is pale and white

But I can't stop now
They still call me fat
Though you can see my ribs

When I think of food
I feel sick
Sick with hunger

I'm going to die
I'm going to hospital
Nurses are pumping me with drugs

Force feeding me
With tubes through my nose
It's not nice

It was OK before they started
But now I'm happy with what I am
Fat

Beth Savage (13)
Bettws Comprehensive School

EARTH!

As I look into the sky
There's something that I realise
We're in a big glass ball.
Floating around we're very small.
We look tiny compared to the rest
We just are the very best.
This earth is not like any other
I don't think there could be another.

Lauren Couch (12)
Bettws Comprehensive School

DISCWORLD

In Discworld all is but quiet,
As the night watch blindly walk around, drunk,
As the dwarfs stumble and get there beards all tangled up,
As rats die in dark alleys.

In Discworld all is very weird
As the Wyrd sisters fly up high, over the forest,
As a Vampire drinks his bubbling blood wine, glass-by-glass.
Served by a, sorba troll!

In Discworld all is so magical,
As Rincewind stumbles over ancient cobblestones,
As little old luggage tails aimlessly on Ricewind's tracks,
As the unseen university spreads its magic.

Discworld is so mystical,
As the psychic shopkeepers confuses customers,
As Dragons appear from mystic caves,
And lost souls fly mindlessly above.

Discworld is so very deadly,
As Death Of Man spreads his mystic cloak over Ankh-morpork,
And Death Of Rat spreads his, not so mystic cloak, over a skull,
Now Discworld is so very confused!

Gareth Jones (12)
Bettws Comprehensive School

HANNAH!

My friend Hannah!
Looks like a spanner
She nags like my mother
She fancies my brother.

My friend Hannah!
Has rosy cheeks
She looks like a rag doll
And she bloomin' reeks.

My friend Hannah
Has hair like straw
She falls and stumbles wherever she walks
She dances and prances around me.

My friend Hannah!
She looks like a spanner
And that is my friend Hannah!

Louise Howes (12)
Bettws Comprehensive School

I'VE GOT A SURPRISE FOR YOU!

I've got a surprise for you!
What colour is it? Is it blue?
Is it square, is it small?
Is it round, is it tall?
Is it a couple of toys?
Is it very, very bright?
Is it dark, as dark as night?
Does it shout, does it sing?
Does it do any of these things?
What is it please tell me?
Open it up and then you will see.

Hayley Morgan (12)
Bettws Comprehensive School

WHO IS THIS?

Creeping towards me,
Was a tall dark man,
Wearing a long black coat,
With fangs.

Sneaking towards me,
Was a funny looking bloke,
With an oval head,
Swinging his long black cloak.

He had sharp fangs,
And long nails,
Then,
All of a sudden . . .
Ahhhh!

Amy Cousins (13)
Bettws Comprehensive School

RHYMING!

I think whatever people say in life
That rhymes comes true . . .
If you own some clocks,
You'll live in a box,
And have a pet fox,
Also wear bright pink socks.

If you have curly hair,
You'll own a cool fair,
Never even care,
And your name would be Claire.

Lucy Marsh (12)
Bettws Comprehensive School

SUMMER FUN HOLIDAY

School ended I was so glad
When it started again I was so sad.
I went on holiday to Lanzarote,
I went in the pool and in the sea,
It was so brill,
I wish I was there still.
I had a great time
And drank loads of wine.
The weather was hot
I like it a lot.
Two weeks have gone and time to say bye.
It's so sad and sly.
Now it's time to go to school
I wish I was back in my pool.

Rachael Edwards (12)
Bettws Comprehensive School

HALLOWE'EN

Hallowe'en is on October the 31st,
People eat sweets and then they burst.
Haribo, cola bottles, chocolate and money,
Vary in flavour from apple to honey.

Little kideos,
Watching their animated videos.
We're upstairs watching Hallowe'en,
Go to bed and have a bad dream.

Scary stories
Over ours.
They watch scary movies
For endless hours.

A ghoul and a ghost,
Running down the street.
Runs into a lamppost
And knocked off his feet.

Still on his feet
His friends down the street
Shouting, 'Hurry up.
Come on let's go and trick or treat!'

Simon Harvey (12)
Bettws Comprehensive School

THE RAIN

The rain
fell like cats
and dogs, but
the man over
the road lightly jogs.
Then suddenly it
turned very bright.
Will that man turn
off his light, it's shining
in my eyes. But I
need to revise!
Like ballet dancers
snow fell, oh dear
I just fell, it
is so slippery
like oil I was
taken to the
hospital like
someone
royal.

Lauren Brown (12)
Bettws Comprehensive School

THE SEA

The sea,
As blue as sapphires.
The waves crashing and curling
on the golden shores.
Like white horses galloping across fields
of golden leaves.
Under the sea, shipwrecks and seaweed
stand still like statues frozen over time.

Adam Levi (12)
Bettws Comprehensive School

THE SUN!

The sun is a steaming fire.
It makes your heart desire.
It is like a diamond shining
in the sky.
If you could only fly.
It is like a gold bottle top
which tells you
when to stop!

Rebecca Jones
Bettws Comprehensive School

WITCHING HOUR

The
witch rode
through the
sky like a monkey
swinging from tree
to tree. Her hat was
as black as night and
as pointed as a
pyramid and as tall as
a traffic cone. A blanket of fog hung over
the ground like a duvet cover on a bed!

Amanda Wray (12)
Bettws Comprehensive School

BURNING FIRE

As the fire is burning bright
Twirling through the starry night.
As the ice is frozen solid
The snow comes down like a blizzard.
As the leaves fall from the trees
Just get blown with the greatest of ease.
As the lightning shoots down fast
Goes straight through like an atomic blast.
From now today and in the past.

Nathan Shepherd (12)
Bettws Comprehensive School

FOOTBALL

On Sundays we play football,
We charge around like bulls,
We come home black as charcoal,
Sometimes I think we're fools.

I passed the ball to Joseph,
He took off like the wind.
The keeper came on out to him,
But Joe still banged it in.

It started to rain badly,
Puddles everywhere.
We were jumping in them madly
But we didn't really care.

Matthew Welsh (12)
Bettws Comprehensive School

BONFIRE NIGHT

Bonfire Night is a time to laugh,
drinks lots of booze until you barf.
Fireworks fly in different directions,
Crackers, rockets in a section.
The bright, bright light, and the jack-in-the-box,
Me, Simon, Jamie and Chris Cox.
Us four boys were drinking beer,
Absolutely nothing to fear.
Mum's drinking Strongbow, Claire's drinking lager
Dad's got his mouth around the beer keg getting fatter and fatter.
4.00am came, the night was over
I'm dreading the morning, I'll be hungover.

David Ramsay (12)
Bettws Comprehensive School

THE OLD WIFE AND THE GHOST!

There was an old wife and she lived all alone,
In an old cottage not far from Hitchin.
She fed her dog in one of the rooms,
But found an old man in the kitchen.

About that kitchen all neat and clean,
The ghost goes pottering round.
And as she got to the top of the stairs,
She suddenly fell to the ground.

The ghost blows up the kitchen fire,
As bold as bold can be.
When the old woman walked into the room,
A naughty old ghost did she see.

He blows on his hands to make them warm,
And whistles aloud, *'Wee-hee!'*
So when her dog ran out of the door,
She forgot to give him his tea.

The ghost tears up and down,
And screams like a storm at sea.
When the old wife went to the shop,
She realised she forgot her key!

Karla Skillern (12)
Bettws Comprehensive School

THE WELSH

The Welsh are known for,
Their choirs and singing,
When they win at rugby,
The bells start ringing.
For the people of *Wales,*
So national, so proud,
With a love of culture,
That's envied throughout.

Charlotte Vigar (12)
Bettws Comprehensive School

THE FIRST GAME OF THE SEASON

It was the first game of the season.
We could see no reason why we were worried
As these big geezers scurried why should be
Hurried?
The ref flicked the coin.
Today Billy had been injured in the groin.
As we ran
As fast as we can
We gained possession
And tried to teach these big geezers a lesson.
It was the second half as we gave a laugh
We were ahead
As they looked half dead
It was full time
We did the team rhyme
They said, 'We'll get you next time.'

Adam Mathlin (12)
Bettws Comprehensive School

TECHNOLOGY TODAY

Technology today
What can we say?
Computers and robots
Science has cured lots.
Surfing the net I'm sure is fun
Can you imagine the
world in 3001?

Ross Yhnell (12)
Bettws Comprehensive School

KING ARTHUR AT WAR

King Arthur on the battlefield,
Shining in the light was his gleaming shield.
He put his hand over his eye,
To see the foe getting closer by.

With Lancelot by his side,
The knights were ready to fiercely ride.
Some of the men were gripping in pain,
But King Arthur had won again.

'Retreat!' yelled the foe and rode away.
'We'll be back another day!'
Arthur rode proudly back,
His knights followed in a pack.

This other day did come again,
This battle was going to be Arthur's main.
He fought tough and was wounded bad,
All of his knights were really mad.

Then eventually Arthur died,
All of his knights really cried.
He had thrown Excaliber into the lake
Ready for the next new king the lady would make.

Benjamin Goldsworthy (11)
Bettws Comprehensive School

My Cat Tiger

My cat
Is a bit fat
But he runs like a jaguar.
He runs as fast as a car,
He runs too fast for me.

He can eat his food as fast as a pig,
He can sleep as long as a bat.
He can leap like a leopard,
He's just too clever for me.

Jennifer Willetts (11)
Bettws Comprehensive School

SEASONS

Warm clothes,
Coloured leaves,
Dragon's breath,
Bald trees.

Blazing sun,
Burnt bodies,
Beaches galore,
Blistering sun.

White snow,
Blazing fire,
Ice rivers,
Snowmen's smirk.

Budding flower,
Babies crying,
Warm mist.

Hannah Parfitt (11)
Bettws Comprehensive School

EYE OF THE STORM

It was ravenous and hungry,
Twisting and turning,
Picking everything up,
And was tipping it upside down.

The storm was swirling around me,
It twisted and turned,
And tossed trees round like leaves.
It had spiralled out of control.

The rain slashed down, flooding the streets,
Echoing on glass
Like shouting in a cave,
Getting their own echoed call back.

A roof from a house was ripped off,
Flew across the sky
And smashed into the ground,
Into a thousand tiny pieces.

Then everything became silent,
Calm, relaxed, peaceful.
The rain had now halted,
Everything was quiet, so still.

Then suddenly the rain lashed down,
The wind whirled round me.
The eye of the storm passed,
The wind, a howling wolf round me.

Sarah Baulch (13)
Bettws Comprehensive School

ALIEN VISIT

An alien came to Earth one day
And decided to look around.
He wandered here and he wandered there,
And wrote down what he found.

'First I found a heavy box
Filled with people who laughed and jeered,
I pressed a square, to my surprise,
The people disappeared . . .

I pressed a lever on a wall,
A small sun brightly shone.
I pressed the lever once again
And the little light was gone.

I like this place, it seems quite nice,
Well it's okay for a change.
I just can't wait to get back home,
Cos this place is too strange!'

Becky Johnson (13)
Bettws Comprehensive School

MY DAY

Up in the morning at quarter to eight,
Go to the bathroom, mustn't be late,
Wash my face, then quickly dress,
Still me hair is in a mess.
Go downstairs and get my brush,
Always in a mad rush.

Out of the house, running madly,
To meet my best friend called Bradley.
Walking to school, the bell rings,
Before I know it I've dropped my things.
RE, science and English have passed,
Two lessons to go, I'll be home at last.

Vicky Howells (14)
Bettws Comprehensive School

THE SNOW SPIDER

The snow spider is white,
It is very, very bright.

The snow spider can give
You a cold, cold shiver.

It's as if when it's cold,
The patterns are bold.

The intricate patterns are like ice,
Which is very, very nice.

Sasha Wainfur (11)
Bettws Comprehensive School

WEATHER

I opened my curtains,
and looked up to the sky.
I watched the clouds
go floating by.
The sun came out
and brightened up the day.
It made it nice
for us to play.
We flew our kites,
in the summer breeze
and watched them dance
above the trees.
The wind blew stronger
and the clouds turned grey.
The rain came down,
and freshened up the day.

Ceri Jones (12)
Bettws Comprehensive School

MATHS

Maths is wicked,
It's really cool
But algebraic equations
Do not rule!

My IQ in maths is really high!
I enjoy it most;
I should win a prize!

Maths is cool!
It's really fun!
But I wish we had a cheeseburger
And a bun!

If we had one of them,
Every day!
Maths would rule
Once again!

I enjoy maths most of all
It's what makes me open
The front door!

Well except my mum!

Gemma Bartlett (12)
Bettws Comprehensive School

SPACE TRAVEL

People travel to outer space,
It is a most peculiar place.
There are galaxies full of stars,
There are planets like Pluto, Venus and Mars.
The sun, the moon and the Milky Way,
There all millions and millions of miles away.
It must be cool in outer space
You can float and fly with endless grace.
Get in the rocket, thrusters on,
Ten to zero and then you're gone!

David Tutton (11)
Bettws Comprehensive School

SLAVERY

Strange white people,
Tearing apart my family,
Treating me like an animal,
Locked away, no light.
The smell of rotting flesh, of
Excrement, of death.
No life for a human being.

On a boat for months,
Hosed down every other day,
No life for a human being.

Alex Coggins (13)
Bettws Comprehensive School

THE CAR JOURNEY

'Are we there yet?' Mum was being asked twelve times in an hour.
'Be quiet kids!' Mum said, 'You'll wake Dad if you shout any louder.'
Dad stirred a little, grunted and pulled the blanket over his head,
'Oh Mummy give me five more minutes,' in his sleep Dad said.
The children roared with laughter, Mum gave a little smile,
'Not much further to go now kids. Just one more mile.'

'Mum I need to go to the toilet, please can you stop the car?'
'Just hold yourself for a while we haven't got to go far.'
Five more minutes down the road Mum bumped into a tree.
'Mum, Mum drive quickly. I really need a wee.'
'Go inside the forest and go to the toilet over there.
Don't worry no one will see you. There's no one else here.'

We've been in the car for an hour and three times I've seen that post'
'Mum I hate to tell you this but I think we're lost.'
'Go and wake your Father he'll know what to do
If he doesn't wake up we'll have to miss the zoo.'
The children tried for ages to get their father to wake.
'Pour some water on his head and give him a little shake.'

Dad still wouldn't wake up so Mum turned around and headed home
'Children sit down and behave yourselves and leave your father alone.'
We pulled into the driveway and went into the house.
'Leave your father asleep, children be as quiet as a mouse.'
They were inside the kitchen having a cup of tea
When Dad came in, sat down and said, 'Why didn't you wake me?'

Charlotte Howard (13)
Duffryn High School

SPACE

Hubbledy do
What can I do?
I'm floating
without a direction.
I stepped off the bus
without any fuss
and discovered
a brand-new dimension.
The pavement is small
from where I now am
but so is the bus
and the car
and the van
for now I can float like a bean in a can.
I think I have made an invention!
It really is a whiz
walking on air is the biz
to the stars I ascend
like a train on a bend
without wheels
or a seat for protection.
Oh cheesy moon
from Cheddar
just look at the bump on the head
from the Earth
I have come
at the suck of a thumb
and fallen
right out
of my bed.

Gemma Preece (15)
Duffryn High School

IMAGINE OUR DESTINY

What will become of the planet Earth?
Imagine what the future will hold.
Will rivers flow, the sun still rise?
Or will the land be frozen and cold?

Will coastlines collapse and crumble away
And land disappear from sight?
Will the ozone crack allowing the rays
Of the sun to show us their might?

We must wake up in time! Stop this doom!
We cannot kill our Earth.
Its beauty, fragrance, its sounds of life
We must protect its worth.

Mistakes of the past we cannot undo,
But the future is ours to write.
Let's conserve, protect, look after our world,
Make sure our destiny's bright.

Ceri Morris (12)
Newbridge Comprehensive School

THE MILLENNIUM WAR

A millennium is but a second in the
history of the earth,
So much history has taken place since
the last millennium's birth,
Kings and queens have traded places,
New lands have been discovered along
with many new faces,
A thousand battles have been fought,
making millions of people very distraught,
War, mind you, can sometimes be
the mother of inventions,
Many of them came from the best
of intentions.
As the new millennium dawns,
It is clear now that all men are just pawns . . .
. . . of time

Matthew Thomas (12)
Newbridge Comprehensive School

IN THE FUTURE

Metal pushchairs, robot babies,
copper gentlemen, lead ladies.
These robots make a funny 'tink',
and beeping sounds that let them think.

Digital brains, wheels for feet,
plastic food is what they eat.
These creatures are a funny race,
but luckily they live in space.

Emily Gilbert (12)
Newbridge Comprehensive School

TRAVELLING THROUGH SPACE

10, 9, 8, 7, 6, 5, 4, 3, 2, 1 blast-off!
Neil Armstrong blasts to the moon,
Maybe the first but maybe the last,
Across the craters tall and small,
See the stars as they fall.

Is there a door to another land?
Will a comet hit his face?
Maybe there's aliens or some kind of life?
All these questions but we see no light.

School trips to Jupiter or to the moon,
Days out at Pluto's park
Rides on Saturn's rings of colour.
Maybe, who will ever know?

Claire Williams (13)
Newbridge Comprehensive School

TIME TRAVELLING

In 1966, England beat Germany with their winning goal.
At the same times lots of miners were employed to dig coal.
Technology has come a long way.
We now have computers, mobiles and Nintendos to play.
In the future there will be no wars
A press of a button and we are all a lost cause.

Lauren Hockey (13)
Newbridge Comprehensive School

ALL THE DAYS GONE BY

Do you ever wonder about the happy days gone by?
The present or the future of the unseen eye?
Do you think about where the world is going,
Compared to what has happened in the past
Or how much longer can our ever-tiring planet last?
Will the end come tomorrow, is it soon but yet so far,
If only he had known the future effect of the car.
Will a monsoon fall or a hurricane blow.
If we all die tomorrow, it has not been in vain
Just think about the happiness that has been
Try to forget the pain.
As I look out of the window
At the ever-lightening sky
I think of all the days gone by . . ..

Rachael Keeble (12)
Newbridge Comprehensive School

THE THREE MILLENNIUMS

In the last 1000 years,
Technology has improved, this is clear.
People once lived in houses made from wood,
And they managed the best they could.

At this very point into time,
People are working 9 till 9.
Money, money is taking over,
And all people are interested in is an expensive Rover.

In the next 1000 years,
People need not shed any tears,
The world will soon be a brighter place,
All because of the human race!

Jessica Gibbons (12)
Newbridge Comprehensive School

ONE DAY

Automatic cars,
will fly you to the stars,
the Earth will be polluted and
world peace will be booted.

All food will come in pills,
but you'll have to pay more bills,
the world will be getting hotter soon,
and we'll be seeing floods in June.

Robots of amazing kinds,
will be taking over our minds.
Don't worry these are just my
thoughts on the future,
But Earth is dying so please
don't abuse her.

Samantha Chivers (12)
Newbridge Comprehensive School

What Will The Future Hold

The future is a mystery
who knows what there will be
from little wooden flowers
to giant metal trees

Maybe there will be countries
which man has not yet found
and little tiny dwarfs
who we will never see around

Or someday the sun might die
to leave a glowing flame
and the world will have shared happiness
where no one is in pain.

Zoe Edwards (12)
Newbridge Comprehensive School

THE PAST!

Christopher Columbus discovered America,
George Stephenson invented the locomotive,
Men and women now have equal rights,
The sexism has gone, the racism will follow.

First there was the swingin' sixties,
Long hair, peace, protests, hippies in dark shades.
The smashing seventies were best,
Platform boots, mini skirts, leather coats and discos.
People did have a right to express themselves freely
Women now have careers something other than being a housewife.

Men stopped working down the coal pits,
The telephone was invented, much to my gladness!
Communication developed,
Finally . . . the year 2000!

Cathy Parker (12)
Newbridge Comprehensive School

TIME

In the past Alexander Graham Bell invented the telephone,
Galileo was the first to say the earth was round,
And Emile Berliner was the one who recorded sound.

At present there is new technology such as the DVD
There is also technology such as the TV
And instead of candlelight we have electricity.

In the future there will not be any environment,
There will only be machinery and instruments,
And the world will be nothing but a load of junk.

Owain Millard (12)
Newbridge Comprehensive School

THE YEAR 2999

There will be cars about in the sky,
People might even be able to fly,
Snails and worms may be able to talk,
Furry fish may be able to walk.

Towns might be covered in glass domes,
You may be able to talk distant without telephones,
The sky will be covered with crystal clouds,
An alien species might even be found.

Kieran Gingell (12)
Newbridge Comprehensive School

THE FUTURE

The future living on planet Mars,
Swimming in golden swimming bars,

Electronic park stands in the way,
Right below the city expressway,

The robot dogs are jumping around,
One penny sweet has gone up to a pound,

The computer worked trees are everywhere,
Where the metal leaves fall in pairs,

Scientists will discover the fountain of life,
People will be queuing up to get a flying bike.

Liam Sheppard (12)
Newbridge Comprehensive School

THE PASTS AND PRESENTS OF AUTUMNS TO COME

Yesterday I still recall,
The woodlands as the shadows fall,
Where creatures hunting on the ground,
Scarcely make a single sound.

Today the smell of autumn weaves,
A memory in the falling leaves,
Of happiness and quiet days,
Where peacefulness and laughter plays.

Tomorrow when the gathering mists,
Something in my heart resists,
I still shall see the future hold,
Another autumn filled with gold.

Curtis Rundle (13)
Newbridge Comprehensive School

THINK

At every moment, someone cries,
Someone's born and someone dies,
Someone laughs and someone sings,
Someone loses, someone wins.

It makes you wonder who you are,
If you'll ever make it far,
Will anyone remember you
When you're gone, when your life's through.

The future is a funny place,
Just like now but slightly changed.
New technologies to use,
More bombs to make, more lives to lose.

There are good and bad things too
In the time ahead for me and you.
We should make the best of what we have
And for what we have we should be glad.

Alison Dennehy (13)
Newbridge Comprehensive School

FUTURE

In years to come there will be
A better life for you and me.
People will be healed by the touch of a hand,
There will be no illness on this land.

In years to come there'll be no war,
Peace will reign for evermore.
Everyone will get along,
Fights and heartache will be gone.

In years to come there will be
No more cars for us to see.
We will be transported there,
Press a button, go anywhere.

In years to come, there will be
Computers taking over me.
There'll be no work for anyone,
Life will be a ball of fun.

Nicholas Lewis (12)
Newbridge Comprehensive School

THE FUTURE

In the future I will live in a rocket that flies all around space,
The planets will all be Holiday Inns,
And the moon will have its own face.

On Earth there will be no telly,
It will be a memory from the past,
It will be like dinosaurs or the two World Wars,
You will learn about it in class.

Animals will have advanced a million and one stages up,
There will be talking dogs, creatures called nogs
And even flying frogs.

Mathew Gajda (12)
Newbridge Comprehensive School

MILLENNIUM FUTURE

Teachers will be robots,
Teaching UFOlogy.
What will happen to English, maths and science,
Now it's Pluto geography.

Dogs will have five legs,
Chickens will start to bark.
Mechanical cats, mechanical birds,
But no more singing lark.

Flying cars and hover bikes,
Maybe spaceships too.
The ultimate hover machine will be,
The Porsche 2042.

I'll really miss my egg and chips,
But alien on toast?
But my knickerbocker glory,
Is what I'll miss the most.

Andrew Rogers (12)
Newbridge Comprehensive School

MILLENNIUMS THROUGH THE AGES

Since long ago back in the past,
Things have changed oh so fast.
We used to travel around on foot,
And people came home covered in soot.

Now this millennium has struck,
This world has come into luck.
For now we travel around in style,
And we can travel mile by mile.

What will our future hold?
Will the world just be sold?
Or will the world end forever?
Forgotten about forever and ever?

Nichola Bryant (13)
Newbridge Comprehensive School

THROUGH THE AGES

Many, many years ago people lived in caves,
The women they were dragged along, often used as slaves.
Egyptian pyramids were being built,
Scottish men began to wear kilts.

Now we have homes with lots of mod cons,
From microwave cookers to hair curling tongs.
The Millennium Dome is quite a mess,
But the London Eye is a real success.

Homes of the future, where will they be?
On earth, in space, or below the sea?
Will there be school trips to planet Mars,
And everyone flying their own space cars?

The future holds a lot in store,
What's behind the secret door?

Ffiona Clark (12)
Newbridge Comprehensive School

MILLENNIUM POEM

What is the past?
Is it when men went reluctantly down the coal mine,
Getting really dirty and losing the track of time,
And never hardly seeing any sunshine,
Or is it what happened yesterday,
Whatever it is it can't happen today,
Because we can't press rewind and then play.

What is the present?
Is it what is happening this day or week,
Like new technology that we are trying to seek,
Or are we at our highest peak,
Maybe the present is what is happening now,
A moment in time for us to allow,
Like at this precise moment that someone might bow.

What is the future?
Is our future world going to be made of metals,
Because we were mean as thorns on nettles,
Now we would have to have holograms for things like petals,
Maybe it won't turn out to be so bad,
Because we might change our attitude and be glad,
Be glad of what we already have and it might not be so mad.

Laura Rees (13)
Newbridge Comprehensive School

2999

Robotic dogs
Chase metal logs
In the virtual park

Tall oak trees
No moving leaves
With no wooden bark

Everything is silver-white
Shining on through the night
Now there is no dark

Religion long forgotten
Bible pages rotten
No longer do the people hark

All animals are dead
Unless they're made of lead
No more singing does the lark.

Hannah James (12)
Newbridge Comprehensive School

THE FUTURE

Desolate buildings stare blindly into space,
Tinged with the memory of the human race.
Purple skies back shrivelled, lifeless trees,
Beside black, polluted seas.

Clouds pass by, thick as lead,
Above a sad land, long dead,
Sand dunes swirl beneath a searing sun, burning red.
A world cursed by a selfish race,
That cut off its nose to spite its face.

Joseph Ashford (12)
Newbridge Comprehensive School

THE YEAR 2058

Trips to the moon and faraway lands,
Aliens and monsters with twenty-nine hands,
No pens or pencils just PCs,
No flowers, no gardens, no rivers or trees,
Helmets and spacesuits would be the trend,
There'd be no telephones, just E-mails to send,
You wouldn't need to queue or you wouldn't need to wait,
This will all be happening in the year 2058.

There would be no buses just flying cars,
That would take you to places such as Venus and Mars,
There'd be no school just home tutors,
You'd do your shopping on your very own computer,
Pets would be run by battery power,
There'd be sweets that would last you up to an hour,
You wouldn't have to come home until late,
This will all be happening in the year 2058.

Lauren Hughes (12)
Newbridge Comprehensive School

THE MILLENNIUM

As we enter a new era we think of the past,
The years seem to fly by really fast.
There have been many battles on land, seas and in the skies,
And many brave soldiers have given their lives.
From the Battle of Hastings to the Second World War,
Many nations have fought from the rich to the poor.

As centuries pass there have been new queens and kings,
In this land of ours there are many beautiful things.
They say there are 7 wonders in this world of ours,
Scientists have even invented electrical powers.
In 1912 the 'unsinkable' sank,
The 1st man on the moon, we've got Neil Armstrong to thank.

To mark the millennium, architects started to build,
The Dome, The Millennium Stadium but would they be filled?
Our hopes for the future are for world peace,
No wars, no fighting and starvation to cease.
For people to be nice in every possible way,
And help one another live in harmony each day.

Hannah Louise Brown (12)
Newbridge Comprehensive School

OUR TIME

If we look back in history to the old times,
With Henry the Eighth and his six wives,
To when Queen Victoria took to the throne,
And both world wars widely known.
In coal mines worked fathers and sons,
They suffered pain but weren't the only ones,
War after war they were bad days,
When none of your troubles would fade away.

There is still a monarchy but Parliament's in control,
It's Tony Blair and Labour against the peril,
We have better schools where we learn more things,
And the punishments are detention not the cane.
On the web, dancing to music or watching TV,
But some lives aren't as good as some can be,
There are charities like Oxfam that help poverty,
This is the new millennium to me.

In the future it's hard to see,
Where you and I may well be,
We'll probably be living on Pluto,
And we'll be covered in silver from head to toe.
There will be no animals and no trees,
Hardly no sound at all no longer the humming of bees,
To get from place to place we'll have flying cars,
And every day and night we'll be under the stars.

Jessica Dee Walker (12)
Newbridge Comprehensive School

FUTURE

Do you ever think of the future,
What the universe might become?
Will we drive around in rockets?
And will aliens become our chums?

Will the earth still have vegetation?
And will money grow on trees?
Will the earth's moon still be there,
And will it be made out of cheese?

What would transport be like,
Would flying a rocket be a breeze?
Would there be traffic wardens,
Or could we do as we please?

Would we still have chop and chips,
Or would we eat alien ribs?
Would we still have farm animals,
Like chickens, sheep and pigs?

Will aliens take over the world,
Or could we all be friends?
How long will we all live?
And what will happen when it ends?

Scott Symons (12)
Newbridge Comprehensive School

THE FUTURE

The future may hold great or bad things,
Wars that could destroy mankind,
Or maybe we'll be friends with beings from a planet made of strings.

In the future there won't be any schools,
Children will wear a hat that will put info into your head,
But beware there won't be any fools.

In the future the Earth'll be no more,
The human race will be on another planet,
And there will be no such thing as a store.

The entertainment systems will be so powerful,
If we are not careful the world'll be taken over by artificial intelligence,
And we'll be living underwater.

Sean Price (13)
Newbridge Comprehensive School

Past, Present, Future

Peasants cry for rye,
Greedy lords oppress for wealth,
Battles are fought nearly every day,
To gain freedom and fair play.

People are inventing things all the time,
Atomic bombs that cause destruction,
Genetic mutations which hurt Mother Nature,
No one thinks for the future.

Mankind hangs on the brink of extinction,
On a dying planet and from alien invasions,
The only hope that earth has,
Is the strategically placed galactic stations.

Rhodri Hughes (12)
Newbridge Comprehensive School

THE NEXT MILLENNIUM

In the next millennium there will be no worries,
Neither will there be any strife,
As in the next millennium there will not be any pollution -
Cos in the next millennium there won't be any cars or lorries!

In the next millennium there will be no crashes,
Because we travel about in electric cars
And planes that make no sound!
And in the next millennium there'll be no road rage clashes!

In the next millennium, *yes* there will be school
But they won't teach boring English,
Nor will they teach maths,
Because in the next millennium they'll teach all things cool!

Post Script

Before the next millennium we must all take heed
Of the dangers we humans make,
When litter is dropped on the floor.
By the next millennium we may not be anymore.

Before the next millennium we must all take care,
As we absent-mindedly spray aerosol all in our air,
We must think of our world *before* we do our hair.
So please by the next millennium pray our world's still here.

Please take heed to the words I just said
Because before long, we may just be dead!

Adrian Yemm (12)
Newbridge Comprehensive School

PAST, PRESENT AND FUTURE

King Henry the Eighth and his six wives,
Two got beheaded, but four stayed alive.
Queen Victoria then had the royal crown,
On every picture she always wears a frown.
Electricity is taking over coal and gas,
I wonder if this year will ever pass?
Inventions will soon be flying cars,
Speeding along on their way to Mars.
All the trees will disappear and there won't be any logs,
We'll have cyber pets, cats and dogs.
If it's like this in the future will it be good?
As I ask myself this question, I think it could.

Cerys Barrett (12)
Newbridge Comprehensive School

AUTUMN

Autumn's coming, autumn's here
the nature's changing all around.
The leaves go flying down and down until
they touch the ground.
Crunch, crunch when you walk
looking like a rainbow.
The trees are dying with no leaves,
they have nothing to feed off.
There's just spiky branches wherever you look,
nature's dying all around!

Autumn's coming, autumn's here,
no animals to be found,
they're all tucked up in their beds
prepared for the gusty winds.
The days get darker by the second,
the weather's biting cold,
autumn's coming, autumn's here!

Laura Fry (11)
St Joseph's High School

THE HORRIBLE RULES OF SCHOOLS

I think it is really bad news,
You have to obey the rules
Of the sad, sad schools.

Don't do this, and don't do that,
We sometimes obey,
That's OK,
Sometimes we don't and blood takes its toll.

Cry: children, that's what they do,
I hate it, but it's their fault,
At the end of the day they still push and pull.

They will never learn,
And that isn't a first,
And I think is a curse.

Marc Wilson (11)
St Joseph's High School

Sport Poem

Sport is fun, I play it every day,
You can play sport, home or away.
Tennis and badminton, where you hit the ball high,
It's so good, you should give it a try.

Football, rugby, are games where you kick,
A good pair of boots should do the trick.
Hockey and cricket, you use sticks and bats,
If you do horse riding, you will have to wear hats.

Sport is very good for you,
It keeps you fit and healthy.
You can make a job of it,
And you may get very wealthy.

Lee Drew (11)
St Joseph's High School

THE HOUSE ON THE HILL

The house on the hill,
Is the spookiest you've ever seen.
With shutters banging and creaking
Against the window sill.

You enter through the door,
Slowly walking up the stairs.
Listening very carefully,
When you hear a roar.

You're running back down the stairs,
Not sure where you're going.
Wondering what the roar was,
Perhaps it was a bear!

Out through the door,
Running past the grass,
Jumping over gates,
You can't wait to tell your mates!

Emma Wilson (11)
St Joseph's High School

MIDNIGHT

It's midnight, dong, dong,
Midnight strikes, dong, dong,
It's time for the witching hour,
It's when witches get their power.

Off they fly,
In the moonlit sky,
They're on their brooms,
Vroom, vroom, vroom.

It's midnight, dong, dong,
Midnight strikes, dong, dong,
It's time for the witching hour,
It's when witches get their power.

They make their spells,
Nobody tells,
But for goodness sake,
I don't know what they make!

It's midnight, dong, dong,
Midnight strikes, dong, dong,
It's time for the witching hour,
It's when witches get their power.

When it's now 1 o'clock,
Tick-tock,
They lose their power,
'Til the next witching hour!

Natasha Milliken (11)
St Joseph's High School

MY PERFECT WORLD

As I daydreamed by the rippling waters of the pond,
For a second I saw my perfect world.
As I stared a little more,
I glimpsed the people in my perfect world.

No one lives on the streets,
Hungry and cold.
There are no labourers,
And slaves are not sold.
When minds are opened,
Happy memories unfold.

No one is racist,
There is no such thing as war.
Everyone has a home,
With window, roof and door.
No one is injured, hurting or sore.

Everyone has warm clothes to wear,
With button, hem and seam.
Everyone is friendly,
Working as a team.
I will stand among them,
The creator of this dream.

Emily Rayment (11)
St Joseph's High School

ANGELS

I'd like to be an angel,
flying high above,
watching people going by
is something I would love.

I'd like to play my harp all day,
but I'd have to do my chores,
when St Peter went away
I'd have to do the doors.

After chores there'd be choir,
and we'd practice quite a lot
Gabriel would blow his trumpet
and I'd take centre spot.

When choir practice finished,
we'd go and have our tea,
angel cake and candy floss,
the cook's speciality.

I'd go home to my little cloud,
my halo I'd take off,
I'd polish it and polish it with
my angel dusting cloth.

I'd fold my designer wings away,
and lie upon my bed,
I'd close my eyes and say my prayers
and rest my sleepy head.

Bethan Tempest (11)
St Joseph's High School

OCEAN FEVER

Sometimes the sea is silver and glitters,
Sometimes the sea is black and gives you the jitters,
But when the sea is in between
The dancing ocean fever is seen.

Bip, bop, bip, bop, the music won't stop
Bubbles of ocean has just got the pop.
The sand has the fever and just starts to rumble,
As everyone runs and no one will grumble.

All the fish start to dance
While the dolphins will prance
The octopus starts to spin,
The goblins come out to see what's for dins.

The goblins are out with their evil eyes.
Looking for someone to catch and fry.
As no one is there they'll go back in,
Very unhappy and getting quite thin.

The mermaids come out flipping their tales,
Then all of a sudden one gives a wail,
The sea is now black and not in between,
Ocean fever is over and cannot be seen.

Sarah Appleton (11)
St Joseph's High School

THE MIDNIGHT TRAIN

Past mounds of grass and moorland boulder
Puffing clear steam over her shoulder
Whistling noisily as she passes
Silent miles of wind - bent grasses

Birds twist their heads as she approaches
Stare from the bushes at her smoky-faced coaches
Sheep dogs cannot turn her course
They sleep on with paws across
In the farm she passes, no one stirs
But a glass in the bedroom gently breaks.

Sian Manship (11)
St Joseph's High School

EURO 2000

England's first match was against the Portuguese,
They went two-up and felt more at ease.
But soon Portugal began a great comeback,
England's defence was starting to lack.
After ninety minutes the whistle was blown,
To Charleroi the players were flown.

Charleroi was the place to be,
When England took on their rivals, Germany.
Half time went by with no score,
England fans were crying for more.
In the second half Shearer headed one in,
This great goal gave England the win.

England played Romania for game number three,
But during the match conceded a penalty.
After a while England went two-one ahead,
But conceded two goals although they'd led.
Unfortunately they failed to qualify,
Nevertheless their hopes won't die.

Matthew Bolton (11)
St Joseph's High School

MY CAT

I always see my cat asleep, I wish she was awake,
But when she is not asleep, she is such a headache!
She miaows and scratches, wanting to play,
It does sound quite nice but it's every day!
If I don't play with her she cries and cries,
And it's hard to resist her cute loving eyes.
It starts off calm then it starts to get rough,
It is hard to play with her because it's so tough.
But after a while she goes back to bed,
Retreats to her basket to rest her head.
Soon after it all, this toy will break,
She is always asleep, I wish she was awake.

Gregory Walker (11)
St Joseph's High School

THE CORNISH COAST

I was there lying on the ground as
the wind blew by and the luscious
grass like feathers tickled the back
of my neck.

The waves violently crashed
against the rocks, and the foam
appeared as white as snow.
The water was clear and unique as glass.

The daisies and dewdrops
swayed in the whistling wind,
like a stream flowing through the woods.

The seagulls called and floated by
as the breeze carried them along,
I take a deep breath and here
I am at the coast of Cornwall.

Alex Driscoll (12)
St Joseph's High School

MERCEDES BENZ

My Mercedes Benz's
A thick dark black,
The lovely leather seats,
That's my car.
A state of the art Sony radio,
The sound of the powerful engine,
That's my car.
The shining bright silver alloys,
The silver mounted Mercedes sign,
That's my car.
The speed of the car going
127 miles per hour,
The smooth ride in the car,
That's my Mercedes Benz.

David O'Neill (12)
St Joseph's High School

STARLING

Black ink-pen squawker
Shot with oily sheen.
Music-hall funny walker
Put him down you don't know where he's been.

Dedicated survivor
In his wormy way.
Professional keep-aliver
I say, I say, I say.

Noisy cat frightener
Strutting on window sill.
Slow roof-whitener
Always tops the bill.

Heidi Northover (12)
St Joseph's High School

MY HORSE

As a horse runs through the trees,
All that he ever sees
Is a great big blur whooshing past,
As he's going very fast.
And as he stops and turns around,
All four feet paw the ground,
He stops and kicks and thrashes out,
He'll go again without a doubt.
He's coming up to a big hedge;
He's going to go over the edge.
Whoa, look at him go straight to the floor below,
Wow, he made it in one big leap,
He's going to need a very good sleep.
Now he's heading for the gate,
I think we're going to be late,
But who is that I can see?
Why of course, it's Bethany D.
Of course the horse was not mad,
Why of course very sad,
To be out in his field all day,
He wanted to come to have some hay.

Bethany Davies (12)
St Joseph's High School

BED BUGS

Goodnight, sleep tight,
don't let the bed bugs bite.
Gran's done it again
she is such a pain.

How will I sleep now,
she's told me the tale.
I'll try and I'll try
but I know I will fail.

They're ugly and furry,
some have sharp teeth.
Then I imagine them
giving me grief.

They're biting my toes
and nipping my nose.
I'm scratching my ear
and shaking with fear.

Tomorrow I'll tell her
to kindly refrain
from mentioning bugs,
it drives me insane.

It sets me on edge
and fills me with dread,
as I try to sleep in
my warm little bed.

Sophie Burridge (12)
St Joseph's High School

MONDAY MORNING

It's Monday morning, lesson one,
and none of my homework has been done.
Only four more lessons to go,
but I am already feeling low,
I'm so tired, I don't care,
I just want to snuggle up to my teddy bear,
I wish I could just grow a pair of wings,
but wishing and wanting are two different things!
Maybe I can just sneak out,
but if Miss catches me, she'll shout!
'Get your pens out,' says the teacher,
I can't be bothered, but some kid shouts,
'I can beat ya!'
Is it normal to think like this?
I'll just think of a sunny beach - ah bliss!
Oh no! There's a mummy chasing me.
Quick I need to open the door, where's the key?
Oh that's better I'm in a pool.
This is wicked, I love school it rules!
Then all of a sudden everything goes blank,
And my teacher wakes me up telling off Mr Hank!

Danielle Tyler (12)
St Joseph's High School

A QUICK ENDING

My heart pounds as I race
Across the ground
Chased by a pack
Of drooling, snarling, hounds
The hairs on my back
Right down to my tail
Stand erect I try to scream out a wail
Although I look around
For somewhere to hide
The hounds are too quick, they're soon at my side
Surrounded now
I can do no more than let out a cry
I look at the hounds,
I know that I am about to die
Fear rushes through me, I want to be sick
I close my eyes
And hope that the ending will be quick.

Catherine Jones (12)
St Joseph's High School

WHALE

Whale,
my favourite friend,
heaving mountain
in the sea.

Whale,
I heard you grieving,
Whale,
I heard you calling me,
Your everlasting life.

Your cry was like a heartbeat,
dying in the sea.
The sea was never the
same without you -
my favourite friend.

Rikki Cooke (12)
St Joseph's High School

MOTOCROSS

When you rev the bike up
It makes a cool, sweet noise,
When you kick-start it
When you go over wicked ramps
The suspension bounces like a mad man.
The soft red leather seat comfies your buttocks as you land.

Oh motorbike!
Why are you so cool?
I ride on and you day and night.
Fun in all conditions,
On ramps and bumps
on hills and mud,

I feel wicked.

Jordan Bartlett (12)
St Joseph's High School

OPEN YOUR EYES

Look around you in this world,
Look at what's happening,
Smashing glasses on the road,
Haven't you guys yet been told?
You can't do this in our world.

Look around you,
Hanging around on the streets drinking.
You ain't even thinking man.
Look at what you're causing.
You're causing some deep disordering.
I don't even know how to handle this.

Look around you.
This is our world.
This is the world we gotta be.
This is the world our children are gonna see.

Look around in this world.
Have a look
At what you're making
This place out to be.

Look around you.
Drugs,
  Drinking,
    War,
      Fighting,
        Hurting,
      Abandoning,
    Hurt,
Abuse.

There ain't no excuse.
You just need to stop.
Stop what you're doing
And look.
Look around you.

Mariam Bidhendy (13)
St Joseph's High School

MISSING YOU

I missed you today when the sun came up
And the sun's rays crept in to say hello.
I missed you today when I took my cup
I drank my tea, ate my toast, feeling mellow.
I missed you too at work when you weren't there,
And felt miserable thinking you were ill.
I missed you at lunch time, and I felt bare,
Spent my time staring out the window sill.
I missed you on the bus journey to home,
Wondering if you would take time to call.
I missed you when I didn't hear the phone,
And wondered if you missed me too, at all.

Is missing you really just a folly,
When I spend my day feeling melancholy.

Deborah Forrester (13)
St Joseph's High School

THE FORBIDDEN CLASSROOM

Two classrooms quite unlike in atmosphere,
In fair St Joseph's (where I write this down.)
Where children shout to and fro, to make things clear,
And look across with a devious frown.
Where teachers try to keep things calm,
Between the classroom of truth unknown.
But nothing ever seems to be calm,
Between the classroom never shown.
The fear in amongst those who pass,
The classes that breathe the forbidden air,
But the truth about the loudest class,
Is something that teachers, all look at in despair.
So whenever you're the visitor next time round,
Remember to wrap up safe and sound.

Michael Beirne (13)
St Joseph's High School

IS IT PARADISE?

One tiny step to pure paradise,
One gigantic leap for Willy Wonka.
Rows like towering tropical palm trees
Are shadowing over your excited body.

The most angelic heavenly scent,
Is weaving through the mundane air:
Like a first class one-way bus route
Driving directly into your confused senses.

A beautiful, radiant rainbow is standing proudly before you.
A jealous traitor of a soldier is concealing your desired pot of gold.
The exact one you have endlessly dreamed and longed for.
Is it there, ready to pour into your trembling, addicted hands?

Fiery imaginations and watering mouths are running wild,
Greedy grubby hands are snatching huge trolleys in an ecstatic race.
An aggressive possessive scoop is piling your wish
Into vast painted paper bags, with all the room in space.

Does there have to be an end to such delightful sweetness?
Or, is this an everlasting fairytale dream?
Will I wake up one day
And find that I'm in a 'perfect' chocolate heaven?

Sarah Carr (13)
St Joseph's High School

MOTORBIKES

If I was a professional motocross rider
like Jeremy Magrath,
I would be the best.
As I stand there with the bike,
as I wipe the sweat
running down my neck,
I leap in the air,
kick my sore leg down and
the roar from the bike and from the crowd
as I look down at the ground,
nervousness runs in my blood,
bang goes the gun and off we run,
wheels spinning away,
trying to balance the bike
as I turn the wet, muddy corners
as I hit a huge jump with a big bump.
One lap to go, phew, what a relief.
I'm in first position and beginning to feel the heat.
We come to the last straight,
people are catching up, then
my power-band cuts in.
I run in first position and that would be
if I was Jeremy Magrath.

Shane Laida (13)
St Joseph's High School

BEST FRIEND 'TIL THE END?

You think you've got the better of me,
Well . . . maybe it is true,
But how can you expect me to be even civil with you,
After all those things you do?
What happened to the friend I adored,
The one who was always there?
What happened to that faithful one,
Who cared deeply for my welfare?
I remember all those great times we had,
Though distant they are now,
I don't even know what brought on this beastly change,
Though I've wanted to ask you how.
And yet now you push me below you,
In the hierarchy of our life,
I do everything that *you* say,
And receive nothing but pain and strife.
You've torn me up deep inside,
And left my feelings for dead,
Yet however much I want to stand up to you,
I keep quiet, and just hang my head.
You've dug my life into a deep, black trench,
There is no easy way out,
And no matter how much I cry for help,
No one can even hear my shouts.
Just because of your tempestuous attitude,
No one will ever come near me,
And if they even speak a word,
You blast them with abuse and profanities.
But the truth is deep down inside,
I want to break loose from your chains,
But now you've held me down for so long,
I fear I may never get up again.
You've held me back from all I have wanted,
My head hangs low in shame,

Why can't I be the person I want to be,
And achieve what I want to attain?
So now it is time for me to go,
And to leave your cruel, menacing side,
I may be alone, all by myself,
But at least I'll have my pride.
You lock me up like a prisoner,
Though I am meant to be your best friend,
It may seem like a game now, but tell me. . .
What happens in the *end* . . .

Joanne Davies (13)
St Joseph's High School

THE MATHS LESSON

We all entered wearily, anticipating the lesson ahead,
Then gasped, my homework, I was dead!
I took my seat, and started to panic, you should always do your maths!
Wait a minute I thought, maybe I could do it in class!

Yes, what a great plan. Simple enough,
Of course, the homework wasn't easy, it was really tough!
I started to struggle, find the value of x, y and z!
I just couldn't get this all through my head.

Of course I should have seen,
Just how terrible could one plan have been?
She wouldn't let me get away with this,
For she was the dreaded, feared, Miss!

'Stephens,' she screamed. 'Not doing your homework I hope'
What could I do? 'Um, well, er, ye see, um.' I just could not cope.
Her nostrils flared and her eyes went wide,
I was so scared. I swallowed hard, I needed to hide!

She looked to the front of the class,
'Now' she said, 'time for maths.'
On the board she wrote some sums,
All of a sudden a boy begins to hum.

She spun round and grabbed the lad by the tie,
Yanked him over the desk, he was one unlucky guy!
He was thrown out of the door followed by Miss. She yelled
'Now then . . .'
The young boy was never seen again!

She walked back in; the room was dead,
One girl was using the wall to rest her head.
Miss grabbed a ruler and hurled it at her head,
It was expertly accurate, and the girl fell dead!

She had the class working, quite and still,
She looked up at me and said, 'You boy, Master Hill.'
'Stephens,' I corrected, 'Don't cheek me lad' she growled
'Up here now!' she said and scowled.

'Your homework, where is it?' she enquired.
Someone in class spoke, she picked up her staple gun and fired!
'Good shot,' she praised herself, 'Now Stephens, you maths' she said,
I couldn't think of anything. She was going to have me bled.

Well, that was going to be the end,
When suddenly I was helped out by an old friend,
I heard a shrill ring. Miss bellowed 'Fire bell!'
Thank God I thought. Saved from my maths hell!

Daniel Stephens (13)
St Joseph's High School

GRANDAD

I walk through that battered old door, once more,
And I see you sitting there,
Your eyes so deep, so full of the past,
They turn, and greet me thus.

I meet with your eyes and look, not see,
Distant memories eroded by your deep, inner pain,
You weep inside yet shed not a tear,
Just look what cruel fate has done to you.

Sitting as you do, your back lurched forward,
In that metal frame; a wheelchair in which you sit,
You need not a university qualification,
To take note of your missing right leg.

You've lost so much weight since I saw you last,
Lost all of your life; no more your large jolly stomach,
It's gone, I know I shan't see it again;
The you that for thirteen years I grew up with.

Hospitals did their best for you,
Medicine had done all it could,
But the best of course, is not good enough,
You don't know, you don't want to know what is killing you.

It is taking you away, grandad of mine,
I know I am soon to lose you,
You will meet your maker, so I'm told,
And I am quite sure of that.

I don't want you to leave me, Grandad,
I don't want you to leave my thoughts,
Man to man, I never could admit it,
But deep inside, I need to proclaim:

I love you Gramp, how much I do,
I know nothing could tear us apart,
Not even in death, I shall not leave you,
I love you too much to do that.

I don't know what to do, Granch,
I long to see you all day, every day,
Should I remember you as you once were?
Or as you are now; in pain, in hell, in misery?

I see you in your wheelchair,
I aided you to your bed; for you to take a nap,
But as I left your new downstairs bedroom,
You held tight my hand; and I shed a tear.

But when that fateful time does come; Grandad,
I know this is what I shall regret,
I will think about what I should have said and done,
To change that, it will be too late.

I kiss you goodbye, on your wrinkled, ageworn face,
Seventy-eight is one fine age to live to,
But as I leave and close the front door,
I stop; take a breath; close my eyes;

I may not return to see you again,
By then you may have gone,
But mark my words, dear old Grandad,
My memories of you will live on.

Thomas Walker (13)
St Joseph's High School

CRICKET

I love the beauty of cricket;
The patience and agility,
The pace and speed of the man and the ball,
The agility of the slide and the drive,
The amazing catches that look so impossible to manoeuvre.

I also love the power of the throw
And unbelievable speed and movement that go against
The laws of science
I love the amazing timing and power
The wait for the right moment to strike
The sixes, the fours, even the singles, move me.

David Whitfield (13)
St Joseph's High School